Easter

Nancy Dickmann

Heinemann Library
Chicago, Illinois

www.heinemannraintree.com
Visit our website to find out more information about Heinemann-Raintree books.

To order:
☎ Phone 888-454-2279
🖳 Visit www.heinemannraintree.com to browse our catalog and order online.

Edited by Sian Smith, Nancy Dickmann, and Rebecca Rissman
Designed by Steve Mead
Picture research by Elizabeth Alexander
Production by Victoria Fitzgerald
Originated by Capstone Global Library Ltd
Printed and bound in China by South China Printing Company Ltd

The content consultant was Richard Aubrey. Richard is a teacher of Religious Education with a particular interest in Philosophy for Children.

14 13 12 11 10
10 9 8 7 6 5 4 3 2 1

Library of Congress Cataloging-in-Publication Data
Dickmann, Nancy.
  Easter / Nancy Dickmann.
    p. cm.—(Holidays and Festivals)
  Includes bibliographical references and index.
  ISBN 978-1-4329-4048-5 (hc)—ISBN 978-1-4329-4067-6 (pb)
  1. Easter—Juvenile literature. I. Title.
  BV55.D525 2011
  263'.93—dc22
                                        2009054304

Acknowledgments
We would like to thank the following for permission to reproduce photographs: Alamy pp. **10** (© Mikael Utterström), **13** (© Image Source), **20**, **23 middle** (© Anonymous Donor); Corbis pp. **4** (© Bob Sacha), **5**, **23 top** (© Jutta Klee), **7** (© Brooklyn Museum), **8** (© Fine Art Photographic Library), **9** (© Elio Ciol), **15** (© Fermin Cabanillas); Getty Images pp. **12** (Chris Graythen), **21** (Barbara Peacock/ Taxi); Photolibrary pp. **14** (ColorBlind/White), **16** (TAO Images Limited), **17** (Mark Edward Smith/Tips Italia), **18**, **23 bottom** (Paul Harris/John Warburton-Lee Photography), **19** (Juergen Richter/LOOK-foto); Shutterstock pp. **6**, **11** (© CURAphotography), **22 top left** (© 2happy), **22 top middle** (© Lobke Peers), **22 top right** (© Pierre Yu), **22 bottom left** (© Elena Schweitzer), **22 bottom right** (© Joshua Lewis).

Front cover photograph of Easter eggs reproduced with permission of Corbis (© Milk Photographie). Back cover photograph reproduced with permission of Alamy (© Anonymous Donor).

We would like to thank Diana Bentley, Dee Reid, Nancy Harris, and Richard Aubrey for their invaluable help in the preparation of this book.

Every effort has been made to contact copyright holders of any material reproduced in this book. Any omissions will be rectified in subsequent printings if notice is given to the publisher.

Contents

What Is a Festival? 4

The Story of Easter 6

What Happens at Easter? 12

Look and See 22

Picture Glossary 23

Index 24

What Is a Festival?

A festival is a time when people come together to celebrate.

Christian people celebrate Easter in the spring.

The Story of Easter

Christian people believe Jesus is the son of God.

Jesus taught people to be kind
and peaceful.

Some leaders did not like what
he taught.

Jesus was killed.

Christian people believe Jesus
then came back to life.

They believe this shows God's love
for them.

What Happens at Easter?

Before Easter, some people celebrate Mardi Gras.

pancakes

They eat the foods that they plan to give up for Lent.

Lent lasts for 40 days. Lent is a
time to think and pray.

On Good Friday, people remember the day Jesus died.

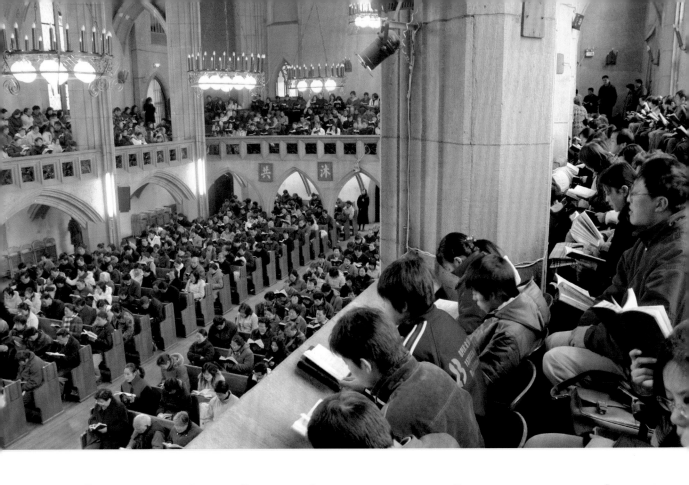

On Easter Sunday, people remember
the day Jesus came back to life.

Some people sing happy songs
in church.

Some people watch Easter parades.

Some people light special candles.

Some people decorate
Easter eggs.

Eggs are a sign of new life.

Look and See

candle

chick

cross

eggs

rabbit

Have you seen these things? They make people think of Easter.

Picture Glossary

 **Christian people** people who follow the teachings of Jesus

 **decorate** to make something look nice by putting colors or patterns on it

 **parade** a line of people, walking along to celebrate or remember something

Index

Easter Sunday 16   Good Friday 15
eggs 20, 21, 22   Jesus 6–10, 15, 16
God 6, 11   Lent 13, 14

Note to Parents and Teachers

Before reading

Ask the children if they know what holidays and festivals are. Brainstorm a list of festivals. Look at which festivals on the list are religious together. Christian people, who follow the religion of Christianity celebrate Easter. Some children from non-Christian or non-religious families may also celebrate Easter in a secular way.

After reading

• Show the children photos of Easter eggs from different cultures, such as Ukrainian pysanky, or even jewelled Fabergé eggs. Ask which symbols and decorations they might expect to find on Easter eggs. Help the children to design their own Easter eggs.

• Explain that Lent is the period of 40 days which comes before Easter. It is a season of reflection and preparation. Lent is often marked by fasting. Ask the children if there are things that they would find it hard to go without. Suggest they choose something (such as computer games or snacks) to give up for a day or a week. Afterwards, discuss what it was like to go without something they wanted.

• Discuss some of the pre-Lent celebrations around the world, such as Fat Tuesday and Mardi Gras carnivals. Explain that these celebrations arose out of the need to use up foods that were not allowed during Lent. Help the children to make pancakes.